# JOKES FOR FUNNY KIDS

9 Year Olds

BUSTER BOOKS

## Illustrated by
# Andrew Pinder

## Compiled by Jonny Leighton
## Edited by Zoe Clark
## Designed by Derrian Bradder

First published in Great Britain in 2023 by Buster Books, an imprint of
Michael O'Mara Books Limited, 9 Lion Yard, Tremadoc Road, London SW4 7NQ

 www.mombooks.com/buster    Buster Books    @BusterBooks    @buster_books

A CIP catalogue record for this book is available from the British Library.

ISBN: 978-1-78055-964-3

1 3 5 7 9 10 8 6 4 2

This product is made of material from well-managed, FSC®-certified forests
and other controlled sources. The manufacturing processes conform
to the environmental regulations of the country of origin.

This book was printed in August 2023 by
CPI Group (UK) Ltd, Croydon, CR0 4YY.

MIX
Paper | Supporting
responsible forestry
FSC® C171272

# CONTENTS

# Introduction

**Why do you not tell jokes to cows?**

They've herd them all before.

Welcome to this te he he-larious collection of the best jokes for 9-year-olds.

In this book you will find over 300 side-splitting jokes which will have you roaring with laughter, from holiday howlers and spy sillies to wacky wisecracks and arty antics.

If these jokes don't tickle your funny bone then nothing will. Don't forget to share the jokes you like best with your family and friends and work on your comic timing!

IT'S ALL IN THE NAME

**What do you call a man who loves exercising?**

Jim.

**What do you call a woman who flies kites?**

Gail.

**What do you call a man that gets scratched by his cat?**

Claude.

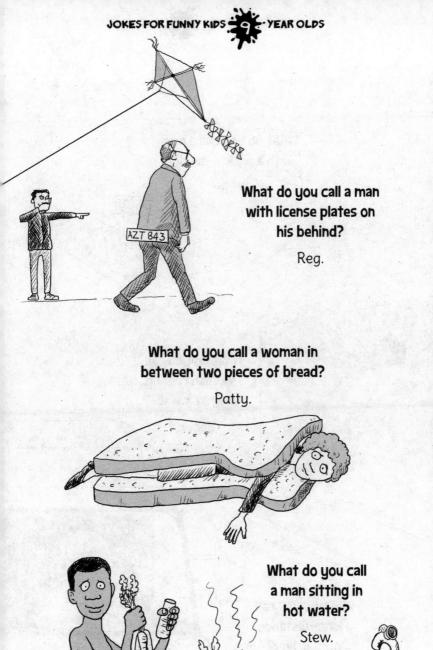

**What do you call a man with license plates on his behind?**

Reg.

**What do you call a woman in between two pieces of bread?**

Patty.

**What do you call a man sitting in hot water?**

Stew.

**What do you call a man with a walkie-talkie?**

Roger.

**What do you call a woman resting against a wall?**

Eileen.

**What do you call a long-distance lorry driver?**

Miles.

**What do you call a boy opening a bag of crisps?**

Russell.

**What do you call a Frenchman wearing sandals?**

Philippe Flop.

**What do you call a girl who loves the beach?**

Sandy.

**What do you call a chef who loves seasoning?**

Rosemary.

**What do you call a man playing the bagpipes?**

Scott.

**What do you call a man who fixes potholes?**

Phil.

**What do you call a goalie between two goal posts?**

Annette.

**What do you call a paramedic in a hurry?**

Nina.

**What do you call a girl who always complains?**

Mona Lott.

**What do you call someone who'd make a great magician's assistant?**

Levvy Tate.

**What did the bride call the groom?**

Marius Quick.

**What do you call someone who's up at the crack of dawn?**

Earl. E. Bird.

**What do you call someone who went to the desert?**

Rhoda Camel.

**What do you call someone who wants a bargain?**

Lois Price.

What do you call
a girl with a snail
on her head?

Shelley.

What do you call two
guys in the window?

Curt 'n' Rod.

What do you call a teacher
who corrects homework?

Mark.

**What do you call a woman who sings at Christmas?**

Carol.

**What do you call a boy with a bug in his hair?**

Anton Head.

Finish

**What do you call a runner racing towards the finish line?**

Harry!

**What do you call a woman with one leg either side of a stream?**

Bridget.

**What do you call a woman standing up straight?**

Nolene.

# BONKERS
# BANTER

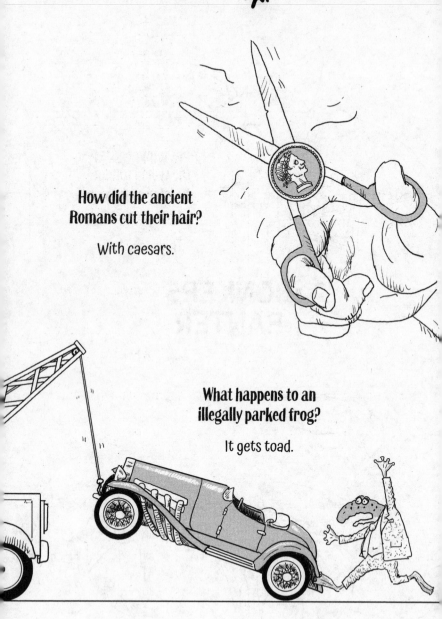

How did the ancient Romans cut their hair?

With caesars.

What happens to an illegally parked frog?

It gets toad.

What happened when the world tongue-twister champion was arrested?

They gave her a tough sentence.

What did the sink say to the toilet?

"You look flushed!"

Why did the spoon cross the road?

He saw a fork up ahead.

**What did the sheep wear to the beach?**

A baa-kini.

**What movie do carrots love?**

The Carrot-te kid.

**Why did the traffic light turn red?**

Because it changed in the middle of the street.

**How can you tell that a giant's really clever?**

They only use big words.

**What can you catch but never throw?**

The flu.

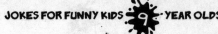

**What's black and white and black and white and black and white?**

A penguin in a revolving door.

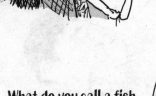

**What kind of haircuts do bees like?**

Buzzcuts.

**What do you call a fish with lots of money?**

A goldfish.

**Where did the spaghetti go to dance?**

A meat-ball.

**What do you call a fish in a movie?**

A starfish.

**What fruit do twins like best?**

A pear.

**What subject do birds love?**

Owl-gebra.

**What kind of fruit loves to swim?**

Watermelon.

**What did the police officer say to his belly?**

"You're under a vest!"

**What do you call a train with a cold?**

Atchoo-choo train.

**What kind of music do geologists love?**

Rock.

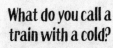

25

**Why do people love telling jokes to eggs?**

They always crack up.

**What type of jokes do pizzas like best?**

Cheesy ones!

**How did the hairdresser win the race?**

She knew a short cut.

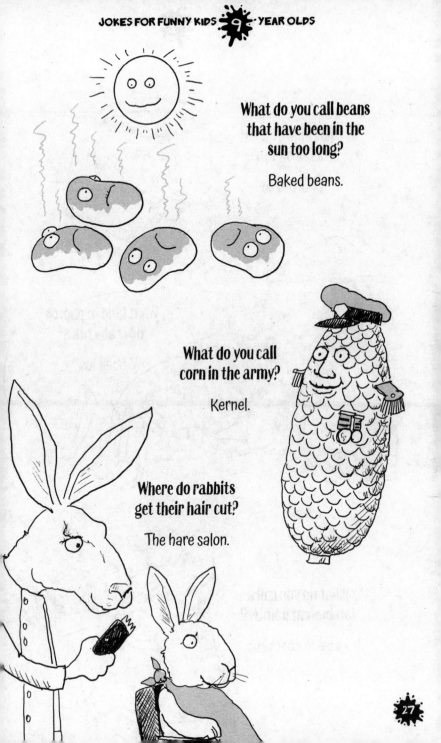

What do you call beans that have been in the sun too long?

Baked beans.

What do you call corn in the army?

Kernel.

Where do rabbits get their hair cut?

The hare salon.

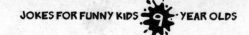

**What kind of treat is never on time?**

Choco-late.

**What kind of photos do crabs take?**

Shellfies.

**What do you call a famous cat painter?**

Pablo Purrr-casso

## Have you heard the joke about the spy?

You shouldn't have, it's top secret!

WE MEET AT LAST, MR POND.

## What do you call a spy underwater?

James Pond.

## What do spies do at bedtime?

They go undercover.

JOKES FOR FUNNY KIDS 9 YEAR OLDS

## What type of footwear does a spy wear?

Sneakers.

## What do you call one cow spying on another cow?

A steak out.

## What do you call a spy in the bath?

Bubble-oh Seven.

## What do you call a spying crocodile?

An all-investi-gator.

## Did you hear about the undercover tarantula?

She was a spy-der.

## I think my vacuum cleaner is spying on me ...

... It's been gathering dirt for years.

**How does Santa know if you've been good or bad?**

He uses mince spies.

**What do spy frogs use to hack computers?**

Rib-bots.

**What do you call a medieval spy?**

Sir Veillance.

What game do undercover
agents love to play?

I spy.

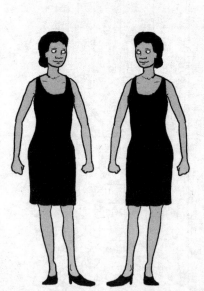

Did you hear about the spy
who played the piano?

He's very low key.

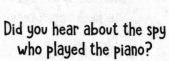

What do you call
spying twins?

Double agents.

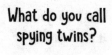

## What spy movie do dogs like best?

Mission Im-paw-sible.

## Did you hear about the undercover amphibian?

It was in-frog-nito.

## What do you call a spy who bleaches his hair?

James Blond.

**What do you call a polite spy?**

A gent.

**Why do pilots make such good spies?**

They're always in de-skies.

**Why do spies like to spend time at the beach?**

Because the coast is clear.

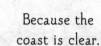

## Did you hear about the spy who liked Italian food?

He was an im-pasta.

## Why do spies stay inside on windy days?

They don't want to get their cover blown.

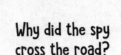

## Why did the spy cross the road?

She didn't, she was never really on your side.

## Why are ducks bad spies?

They quack under interrogation.

## Did you hear about the baker who has some top secret information?

It's on a knead-to-know basis.

## What do deer use to communicate undercover?

Moose code.

Did you know that dogs make for great spies?

They're always digging up dirt on people!

How do you spy on a zookeeper?

Tap their phone lions.

What do you call peppers working undercover?

Spice.

What do you call an undercover rodent?

Anon. E. Mouse.

Did you hear about the undercover shoemaker?

She was in-clog-nito.

What kind of spy missions do bees go on?

Sting operations.

ZANY ZOOS

**Why shouldn't you trust a big cat in a game of chess?**

It might be a cheetah.

**Did you know you should never trust the king of the jungle?**

He's always lion.

**How do gorillas get strong?**

On the monkey bars.

42

How do they work out distance in the jungle?

With a measuring tapir.

What happens when you annoy a monkey?

They go bananas.

Which shape do jungle animals like the most?

A tree-angle.

**What did the farmer say when she lost one of her cows?**

"I made a miss-steak!"

**Did you hear about the magic tractor?**

It turned into a field.

**Where do sheep go to get medicine?**

The baa-macy.

**Which farm animal has a key but no lock?**

A tur-key.

**What fruit do scarecrows eat?**

Straw-berries.

**Why do you not tell jokes to cows?**

They've herd them all before.

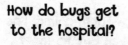

## How do bugs get to the hospital?

In an ant-bulance.

## What do insects learn at school?

Moth-matics.

## What did one firefly say to another?

"Glow away!"

**What kind of bird doesn't need a comb?**

A bald eagle.

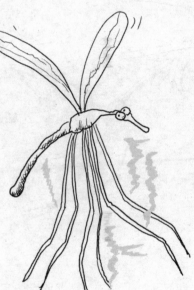

**What do you call a smelly insect?**

Daddy pong legs.

**What's the difference between a fly and a bird?**

A bird can fly but a fly can't bird.

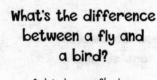

**Why do birds fly south for winter?**

Because they hate taking the train.

**Why do hummingbirds hum?**

Because they can't remember the words.

**How do chickens get strong?**

They do eggs-ercise.

**How did the bird burglar break into the house?**

With a crow bar.

**What do you call a cheerful kangaroo?**

A hop-tomist.

**Why did the turkey cross the road?**

It was the chicken's day off.

**Where did the dog astronaut go?**

The bark side of the moon.

**What do dogs love to dance to?**

Pup music.

**How does a dog get into the house?**

Through the labra-door.

**What did the snake write at the end of the letter?**

With hugs and hisses.

**What kind of socks do grizzlies wear?**

None, they have bear feet.

**Why did the kittens like bowling?**

They were alley cats.

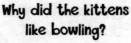

# MYTHICAL MAYHEM

**Which mythical creature always gets lost?**

A where-wolf.

**When do werewolves go trick-or-treating?**

Howl-o-ween.

**Which day of the week do werewolves like best?**

Moon-day.

**How are dragons
so good at music?**

They really know
their scales.

**Why can't dragons
play ice hockey?**

If they breathe fire,
the ice melts.

**My teacher is telling us
about mythical creatures ...**

... It's beginning to drag-on.

**What do you call a scary unicorn?**

A night-mare.

**What kind of jokes do unicorns tell?**

Uni-corny ones.

**How do unicorns get around?**

On a uni-cycle.

How does a mermaid
say goodbye?

"Sea ya later!"

What do mermaids do
on their birthday?

Shell-abrate!

Why did the mermaid
cross the ocean?

To get to the other tide.

**How do you describe an average mythical beast?**

Medi-ogre.

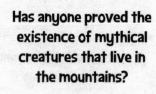

**Have you heard about the mythical cow?**

It's legen-dairy.

**Has anyone proved the existence of mythical creatures that live in the mountains?**

Not yeti.

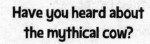

**Did you know that Rapunzel is not a fairy tale?**

It's a hairy-tale!

**What do you call a brainy fairy?**

Thinkerbell.

**Why don't fairies live under toadstools?**

Because there's not mush-room.

**Where do vampires go for a swim?**

The Dead Sea.

**What sport do vampires play?**

Bat-minton.

**How do you know that a vampire has a cold?**

It's coffin.

**What game do monsters play?**

Hide and shriek.

**What's big, furry and has eight wheels?**

A monster on roller skates.

**What do you give a seasick monster?**

Plenty of room!

**What do you call
a small minotaur?**

A mini-taur.

**How do you show someone round a labyrinth?**

With a mino-tour.

**Did you hear about the
grumpy minotaur?**

He's really bull-headed.

**Why did the pharaoh build a statue of himself?**

He sphinx he's the best.

**What did Tutankhamun say about the sphinx painting?**

"It's a monsterpiece!"

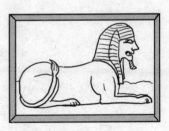

**I told the sphinx it was a terrible swimmer, but it didn't believe me ...**

... It was in de-Nile.

**There's a half-man, half-horse at the zoo ...**

... It's the centaur of attention.

**Where does a half-man, half-horse play tennis?**

On centaur court at Wimbledon.

**I was going to make a joke about a half-man, half-goat ...**

... But it wasn't very faun-y.

# JOLLY JESTERS

**Who even cares about Roman numerals?**

I, for one.

**Why did the tomato stay after school?**

To ketchup on its homework.

**Did you hear about the man who tried to make a belt out of watches?**

It was a waist of time.

66

**What did one bird say to the other?**

"Hello, tweet-heart!"

**What kind of toothpaste does a science teacher use?**

Experi-mint.

**What's worse than finding a worm in your food?**

Finding half a worm ...

**Which animals loves baseball?**

Bats.

**How do you giftwrap a cloud?**

With a rain-bow.

**What did the pirate Dalmatian say?**

"X marks the spot!"

**What music do broccolis like best?**

Broc 'n' roll.

**What do you call a great chicken?**

Im-peck-able.

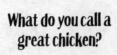

**Why was the strawberry annoyed?**

Because it was in a traffic jam.

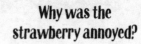

**Where do gherkins go to relax?**

Trop-pickle islands.

**Why did the mermaid leave school?**

Her grades were below C level.

**What do cats have for dessert?**

Cake and mice cream.

**How do you stay warm in a room?**

Go to the corner, where it's always 90 degrees.

**What has sixty feet and sings?**

The school choir.

**What did the banana say to the dog?**

Nothing, bananas can't talk.

**Where do New York pigs live?**

Sty-scrapers.

**What do you call the queen of cows?**

Your Moo-jesty.

**How do penguins finish a race?**

They peng-win.

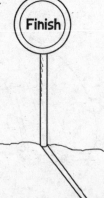

**What noise do hedgehogs make when they cuddle?**

OUCH!

**How did the pirate buy his ship?**

On sail.

**How do cats make whipped cream?**

With a whisk-er.

**Who's the most famous French skeleton?**

Napolean Bones-apart.

**Are black cats bad luck?**

Only if you're a mouse.

**Why was the calendar afraid?**

Its days were numbered.

**How much does it cost to park Santa's sleigh?**

Nothing, it's on the house.

**Why did the carrot go to the hairdressers?**

Its roots were showing.

**What do polar bears eat for dinner?**

Iceberg-ers.

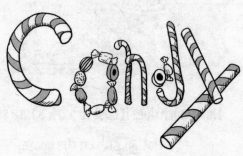

**Which two letters spell 'candy'?**

C and Y.

**Why can't you trust tacos?**

They always spill the beans.

**How do bees keep their breath fresh?**

Bumble gum.

**What's small, black and yellow, and drops things?**

A fumble bee.

**Where do fish sleep?**

The river bed.

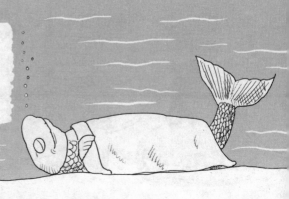

**What has four wheels and flies?**

A garbage truck.

## What kind of car does an electrician drive?

A Volts-wagon.

## Who won the race between shoelaces?

Nobody, they tied.

## Why did the girl throw the clock off the roof?

She wanted to see time fly ..

**What's the coolest thing at a birthday party?**

Ice-cream.

**What do farmers do at birthday parties?**

Turnip the beet!

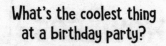

**What do monsters serve at their birthday parties?**

I scream cake.

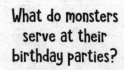

**Where do insects go to relax?**

A bee and bee.

**Where do rabbits go to catch a flight?**

The hare-port.

**Why don't elephants need suitcases?**

They already have trunks.

What did the parasol
say to the beach towel?

"I've got you covered."

What airline do
vampires like best?

British Scare-ways.

Why did the campsite
manager quit?

It was too in-tents.

## Why did the robot go to the beach?

To recharge her batteries.

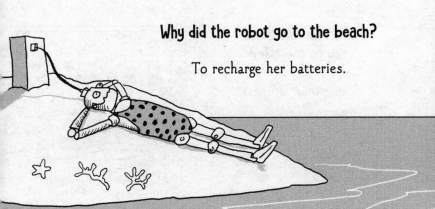

## What city do cows love to visit?

Moo York.

## Where did the algebra teacher take a trip to?

Times Square.

**What did the beach say to the tide?**

"Long time, no sea!"

**What did one sand dune say to another?**

"I will never desert you."

**Why did the detectives turn up at the beach?**

Something fishy was going on.

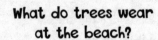

**What do trees wear at the beach?**

Swimming trunks.

**How do you say hello at the beach?**

With a sand-shake.

**What does Cinderella wear at the beach?**

Glass flippers.

**What do you call a penguin in the Sahara?**

Lost.

**Why did the banana wear sunscreen on the beach?**

So it didn't peel.

**Why did the apple pie cry on Thanksgiving?**

Its peelings were hurt.

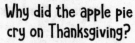

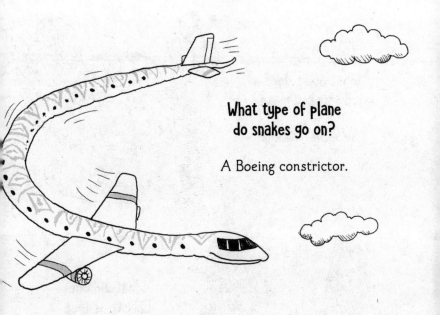

## What type of plane do snakes go on?

A Boeing constrictor.

## What do you get when you drop a pumpkin on Halloween?

Squash.

**What noise does a jelly turkey make?**

Wobble, wobble.

**What did one Christmas tree say to the other?**

"Lighten up!"

**How do Christmas trees get their emails?**

They log-on.

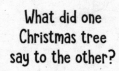

**What do Spanish sheep sing at Christmas?**

Fleece Navidad.

**Where do phantoms buy their Christmas dinner?**

At the ghost-ery store.

**What did the peanut butter say on Christmas Day?**

"'Tis the season to be jelly!"

What's brown and hairy and wears sunglasses?

A coconut at the beach.

Why don't fish ever take a break?

Because they're always in school.

Where does stationery go during the summer?

Pencil-vania.

PLANET EARTH
PUNCHLINES

**Where do spiders learn geography?**

On the web.

**Did you hear the joke about the mountain?**

You'll never get over it.

**Which relative do penguins love to visit?**

Aunt Arctica.

**Why are maps like fish?**

They both have scales.

**Why did the map get told off?**

It had a bad latitude.

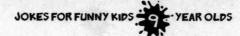

**What do you find
in the middle of
the ocean?**

The letter e.

**What do you call
an island filled
with cupcakes?**

Desserted.

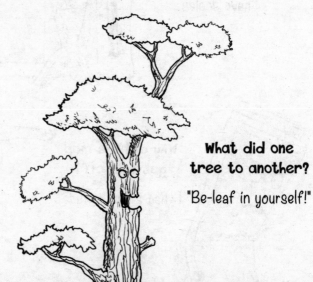

**What did one
tree to another?**

"Be-leaf in yourself!"

**What food do forests like best?**

Mac and trees.

**How did the tree get lost?**

It took the wrong root.

**What's the difference between weather and climate?**

You can't weather a tree but you can clim-ate.

**How do plants greet each other in spring?**

"Hey bud!"

**How do mountains see?**

They take a peak.

**What kind of flowers grow on your face?**

Tu-lips.

**Why did the leaf go to the doctor?**

Because it looked a bit green.

**What has a mouth but cannot eat?**

A river.

**Which landmark
can't eat anything?**

The 'I full' tower.

**What shade
does the wind
love most?**

Sky blew.

**What kind of hair does
the ocean have?**

Wavy.

**Which is funnier: mountain ranges or forests?**

Mountain ranges of course, they're hill-areas.

**How do trees like to dance?**

They sway.

**Which herb takes the longest to grow?**

Thyme.

O-hi-O!

Which US state is round at each end and high in the middle?

Ohio.

What runs but is never out of breath?

A stream.

What's the most expensive place to visit in Spain?

Costa Fortune.

700€

HE

**Why did the fox get wet?**

It didn't check the weather fur-cast.

**Why do little clouds look up to big ones?**

They're the raining champions.

**How do hurricanes see?**

With one eye.

**What gets a year older whenever it rings?**

A tree.

**What game do mountains play?**

Hide and peak.

WACKY WISECRACKS

**What music do chefs love?**

Wok 'n' Roll.

**What does bread say during a game of hide-and-seek?**

"Bready or not, here I crumb!"

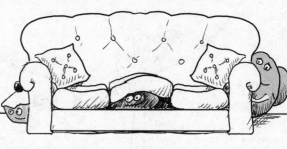

**Why couldn't the lemon cross the road?**

It ran out of juice.

**What do you drink when you're thirsty in dance class?**

Tap water.

**What do you eat when you're cold and angry?**

A brr-grr!

**What do you do if you're hiking and find a fork in the road?**

Stop for lunch.

**What's faster, hot or cold?**

Hot, as you can easily catch a cold.

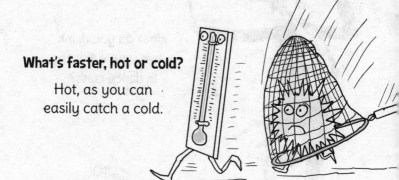

**Why was the cucumber mad?**

It was in a pickle.

**What did the triangle say to the circle?**

"You're pointless."

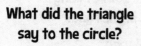

**Why was the mushroom always invited to parties?**

Because he's a fun-gi.

**Did you hear about the thief that stole a calendar?**

He got a year.

**What kind of dance do cows do?**

The milk-shake.

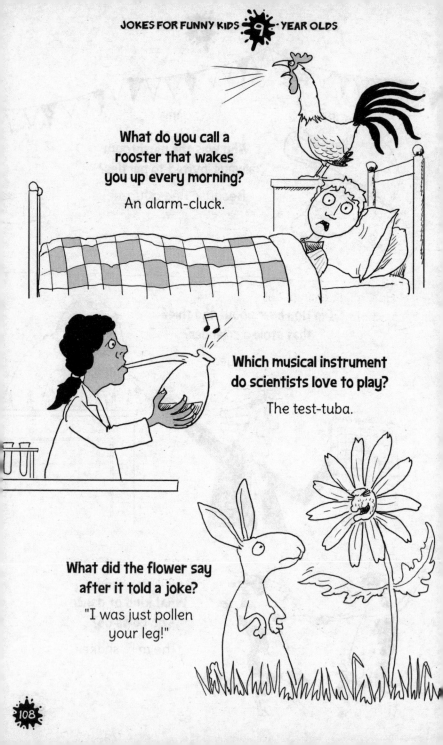

**What do you call a rooster that wakes you up every morning?**

An alarm-cluck.

**Which musical instrument do scientists love to play?**

The test-tuba.

**What did the flower say after it told a joke?**

"I was just pollen your leg!"

**What game do sharks love to play?**

Swallow the leader.

**How much change do you get for a skunk?**

One scent.

**How do you know when a cookie is happy?**

It gives you the crumbs up.

**Which ballet do
ducks love the most?**

The Nut-quacker.

**What does a skunk sing
on Christmas Day?**

Jingle smells.

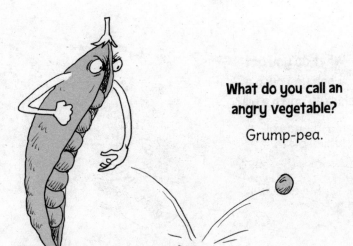

**What do you call an angry vegetable?**

Grump-pea.

**What dog is always on time?**

A watch dog.

**What room can nobody enter?**

A mush-room.

**What do you get when you push a chicken down a hill?**

An egg roll.

**Who wears shoes while sleeping?**

A horse.

**How do trees contact each other?**

By te-leaf-one.

**What does a spider wear to get married?**

A webbing dress.

**Why did the farmer plant money?**

To make her soil rich.

**Why did the robot go to the shoe shop?**

To get rebooted.

**Why did the police arrest the chicken?**

It was suspected of fowl play.

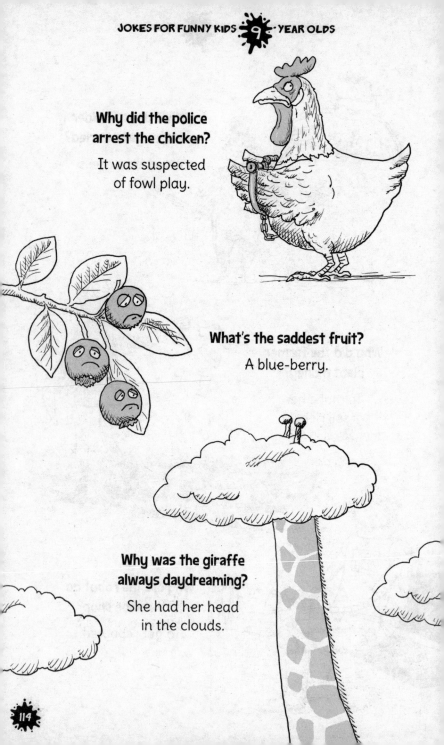

**What's the saddest fruit?**

A blue-berry.

**Why was the giraffe always daydreaming?**

She had her head in the clouds.

**What do you call an octopus who loves music?**

A rocktopus.

**What cheese do monsters love?**

Zom-brie.

**What do you use to fill up an orange car?**

Juice.

**How does a monster
count to 100?**

On its fingers.

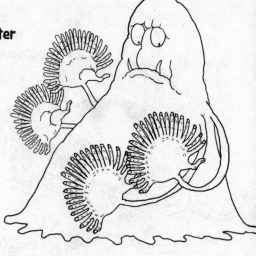

**What do lipstick and mascara
do after they fall out?**

Make-up.

**What did the princess
say when the prince
ate her ice cream?**

"How dairy!"

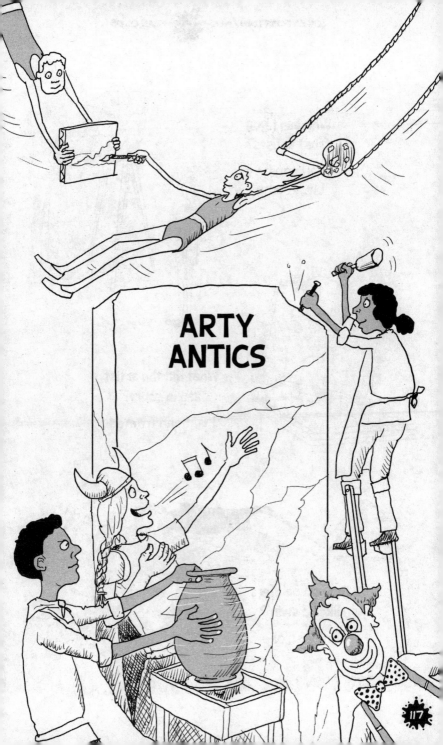

ARTY
ANTICS

**Why can't you trust artists?**

They can be a bit sketchy.

**What did the artist say in court?**

"I've been framed!"

**How do painters like to swim?**

Brushstroke.

## What do dogs love to paint?

Paw-traits.

## Did you hear about the artists who got married?

It was pig-ment to be.

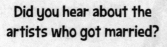

## How do potters say goodbye?

"Let's clay in touch!"

**Did you hear about the banker who loved art?**

She had loads of Monet.

**Which famous painting is always whining?**

The Moan-a Lisa.

**Why did Van Gogh become a painter?**

He didn't have an ear for music.

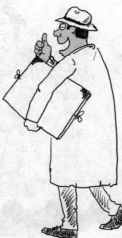

**How do painters greet each other?**

"Yellow!"

**How did the artist warm up his painting?**

He put on another coat.

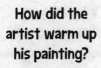

**Did you hear the joke about the broken pencil?**

It's pointless.

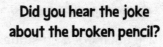

**Did you hear about the boy who wanted to be an actor?**

He was just going through a stage.

**Why are play audiences so sad?**

They're always in tiers.

**Did you hear about the farmer who liked acting?**

He got mooed off stage.

**Why are movie stars so cool?**

Because of all the fans.

**What do you call a movie about a superhero that's lost all her powers?**

Super-zero.

CHEDDAR

**Did you see the movie about cheddar?**

It was super cheesy.

EXIT

**Did you hear about the clown that ran away with the circus?**

They made him bring it back.

**I had a friend who used to perform on stilts ...**

... I always looked up to her!

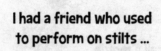

**Did I tell you I used to work for a trapeze artist?**

That was until I got let go.

**Why do people love telling jokes to books?**

They laugh for pages and pages.

**Did you hear about the book of mazes?**

You could really get lost in it.

**Which street do authors live on?**

Writer's Block.

**Why did the pianist get locked out?**

She forgot the keys.

**I keep hearing music coming from the printer ...**

... I think it's jamming.

**Why did the chicken join the band?**

It already had drum sticks.

**Who's the most famous farmyard artist?**

Pablo Pig-casso.

**Who's the second most famous farmyard artist?**

Vincent Van Goat.

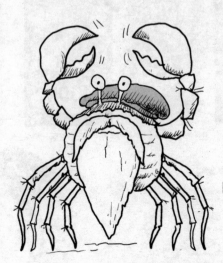

**Who's the most famous artist under the sea?**

Leonardo Da Pinci.

# ALSO AVAILABLE:

ISBN: 978-1-78055-963-6

ISBN: 978-1-78055-626-0

ISBN: 978-1-78055-624-6

ISBN: 978-1-78055-625-3

ISBN: 978-1-78055-965-0

ISBN: 978-1-78055-943-8

ISBN: 978-1-78055-908-7

ISBN: 978-1-78055-907-0

ISBN: 978-1-78055-785-4

ISBN: 978-1-78055-784-7

ISBN: 978-1-78055-708-3